Bird World

by Meredith Phillips

Content Adviser: Professor Peter Bower, Barnard College, Columbia University, New York, New York
Reading Adviser: Frances J. Bonacci, Reading Specialist, Cambridge, Massachusetts

COMPASS POINT BOOKS

MINNEAPOLIS, MINNESOTA

Compass Point Books
3109 West 50th Street, #115
Minneapolis, MN 55410

Visit Compass Point Books on the Internet at *www.compasspointbooks.com*
or e-mail your request to *custserv@compasspointbooks.com*

Photographs ©: Royalty-Free/Corbis/Fotosearch.com, cover; PhotoDisc, 3; Photos.com, 4; Corbis, 6 (left); PhotoDisc, 6 (right); Photos.com, 7; Ingram Publishing, 8; Corel, 9; Photos.com, 10, 11; Corel, 13; Clipart.com, 14; Eric and David Hosking/Corbis, 15; Jack Novak/SuperStock, 16; Photos.com, 17; Corel, 18; PhotoDisc, 19; Network Productions/Index Stock, 21; Frank Siteman/Index Stock, 22/23; Photos.com, 23 (top right); PhotoSpin, 25; PhotoDisc, 26, 27(top left); PhotoSpin, 27 (bottom left); Clipart.com, 28 (top left), 28 (bottom center); Corel, 28 (top right), 28 (bottom right); PhotoDisc, 28 (right center); Clipart.com, 29 (bottom left), 29 (bottom right); Photos.com, 29 (top center); PhotoSpin, 31.

Creative Director: Terri Foley
Managing Editor: Catherine Neitge
Editors: Sandra E. Will/Bill SMITH STUDIO and Jennifer VanVoorst
Photo Researchers: Christie Silver and Tanya Guerrero/Bill SMITH STUDIO
Designers: Brock Waldron, Ron Leighton, and Brian Kobberger/Bill SMITH STUDIO and Les Tranby
Educational Consultant: Diane Smolinski

Library of Congress Cataloging-in-Publication Data
　　Phillips, Meredith, 1971–
　　Bird world / by Meredith Phillips.
　　　　　p. cm. — (Pet's point of view)
　　Includes index.
　　ISBN 0-7565-0700-6 (hardcover)
　　1. Cage birds—Juvenile literature.　I. Title. II. Series.
　　SF461.35.P49 2005
　　636.6'8—dc22　　　　　　　　　　2004004995

"From *my* point of view!"

Table of Contents

NOTE: In this book, words that are defined in Words to Know are in **bold** the first time they appear in the text.

Who Is Your Bird?

Pet Profiles

You and Your Bird

Animal Almanac

From Food to Friend

Rise and shine! This is your wake-up call! There's nothing like a song—or a squawk—from a bird to start the day. We birds are the inspiration behind the alarm clock you use to wake up. It's just one part of the long relationship between people and birds.

Our relationship with humans dates back more than 4,000 years. Originally, we were used for food, but humans soon recognized our qualities as companions. It is not clear when we were first **domesticated,** but Egyptian hieroglyphics depict the first pet birds, including doves and parrots.

Over time, our relationship with humans evolved, but it was not until the 1800s that owning a bird as a pet became truly popular. Small canaries were valued for their sweet, delightful songs and became some of the first **avian** additions to people's homes. Today, most of us kept as pets are small **songbirds,** like canaries, finches, and parakeets. However, larger, more colorful, and exotic birds like parrots, macaws, and cockatiels are also popular.

Birds often have colorful **plumage** with interesting shapes, so you may be drawn to our striking appearance. However, we are very particular pets. Read on, and decide if one of us could be the right friend for you.

5

Birds of a Feather

When you think of birds like me, you probably think of feathers. Feathers are amazing! My feathers must be strong enough to allow me to fly, but they must also be light and flexible. I have two types of feathers: **downy feathers** and **contour feathers.** Downy feathers keep me warm, and contour feathers keep me dry.

In the wild, I must fly to keep myself safe, so my entire body is structured to make flying possible. My wings are rigid, meaning that they do not really bend. They are formed by bones, not muscle. Hollow bones make me weigh less, which makes flying easier. My chest muscles are large, giving me power to beat my wings. You'll notice that I have a large breastbone to hold the muscles I need for flight.

My feet are carefully designed for perching, walking, standing, hopping, or climbing around. The careful arrangement of my four **opposable** toes keeps me steady.

I also use my beak as a foot sometimes because it can help me climb around. I fidget with it when I'm bored and grind the top and bottom parts together when I am sleepy or pleased. I use my beak when I want to be tough with you (or another bird), but also when I want to be tender with baby birds in my care. My beak is designed to help me eat the food I need. Small birds usually have straighter beaks, which are good for closing down on things like seeds or worms. Larger birds, such as parrots, have strong, hooked beaks that can crush a nut.

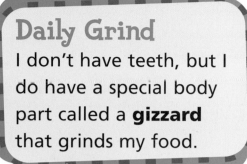

Daily Grind
I don't have teeth, but I do have a special body part called a **gizzard** that grinds my food.

A Bird's Eye View

All animals use their senses to understand the world, and we all see it a little differently. So what does life look like to me—your bird?

Sight: In the wild, I need to make quick in-flight decisions and find tiny pieces of food on the ground from high in the air. My superb eyesight is my best tool. Since my eyes are positioned on the sides of my head rather than in the front, I can see in a far greater **radius** than other animals and humans. My vision also allows me to see more colors than humans.

Hearing: Since you can't see them, you probably think I don't have ears. I do, though! My ears are tucked safely under swirls of feathers. Scratch them. I love it!

My range of hearing is limited, but within the range of sounds that I can hear, I pick up far more detail than you do. I can detect small differences among other birds' songs and can make up some pretty tricky melodies myself. If I am a parrot, I can easily imitate you or the dog.

Taste: I may not have a nose, but I do have a rather amazing beak. My beak is both my nose *and* my mouth. I have a fairly developed sense of taste, and like you, I can taste the differences among things that are salty, sour, bitter, and sweet.

Colorful Companions

Gouldian finch

How many kinds of birds are there? Simply put, far too many to list. For a pet, you will want to narrow down your options to just a few of us.

Finches like me are one bird to consider. I come from Africa and Asia, where I am considered a bit of a pest. Finches like to eat crops, and as a result, people there have tried to get rid of some of us by selling us for pets.

I am a tiny bird, not larger than 4 or 5 inches (10 or 13 centimeters) long, and I live for five to seven years. I am cheerful and easily adapt to my surroundings. I get along well with other birds, but I do not ever become too friendly. I do not talk either, but I am a curious and interested pet with a sweet, cheerful chatter. It is nice to have me around because I am always in a good mood!

If you're thinking about keeping a finch as a pet, there are a number of different kinds of us for you to consider. Zebra finches are good for first-time owners and can be kept in a cage indoors or an **aviary** outside. Males have a black-and-white zebra pattern on the chest and a terrific reddish-orange smudge on their cheeks. Both males and females have orange bills. Melba finches look similar and have a soft, sweet song.

Gouldian finches are more sensitive and need to live indoors, perhaps with a heater. These finches have feathers that are sunny yellow and gold, bright sea blue, light sky blue, and brilliant green. The feathers actually become brighter with age.

Melba finch

Budgerigars

Popular Parakeet

Although I am technically a parakeet, you probably know me better as a budgerigar. Budgies are so popular that we are usually considered as a separate group of birds. Worldwide, we number in the millions as pets. In fact, budgies like me are the most popular pet bird in the world! That is because we are small, inexpensive, and good-natured. We can also mimic whatever we hear. No wonder we are so popular!

Budgies come from Australia. Though we originally were green with yellow and black flecks, we are now bred in a range of colors. There are lutino (bright yellow) budgies and gray-winged, sky-blue budgies. The budgie with the longest name and most unusual look is the crested opaline cobalt budgerigar.

Budgerigars

These birds are bright sky blue with darker blue feathers. The crest refers to the unusual tuft of feathers spraying down over the beak, which, as with all budgies, is a distinctive little stub.

I grow to about 7 inches (18 cm) in captivity—much larger than in the wild. Still, I am a small bird. I have a life span of about seven years.

How Do You Do?
Budgerigars were originally "discovered" by Thomas Watling, who trained his bird to speak. One day Watling's boss came by and was startled to be greeted by a tiny bird asking politely, "How do you do, Dr. White?"

Your Tweety Bird

Among canaries like me there is much variety. We come in fabulous colors and have a wide range of body shapes, from the broad and thick border fancy canary to the more delicate Scotch fancy and Yorkshire fancy canaries. To look at the Norwich fancy canary, you would never know we had eyes! The Parisian frilled canary is hardly recognizable as a bird, with fantastically tufted and fluffy feathers curling up, around, and in all directions. Red factor canaries may be the most spectacular, with a peachy, reddish-gold plumage that changes color depending on diet.

Common canary

What all of us have in common, though, is that we are between 4 and 7 inches (10 and 18 cm) long and live for about 10 years. We are delightful little birds, and male canaries sing lovely songs. Training us, however, is often difficult.

Miner Birds

Canaries like me were once used in mining towns in England to determine if there were poisonous gases or if oxygen was low deep in the mines. Sadly, many canaries died this way, but the contact helped humans learn to appreciate us as pets.

White-bellied canary

Cockatiels and Parakeets

Crests and Colors

I'm a cockatiel! I'm easy to recognize—just look for my crest, the clump of feathers at the top of my head. I can hold my crest upright to look like a fancy hat, but I can also let it down when I am relaxed. I have circular smudges of orange beneath my eyes that look like blush spots on the face of a clown. I am very distinctive looking—and very popular. I am easy to breed and make a good hobby for the growing number of people becoming interested in keeping birds. I am cheerful, affectionate, good-looking, and easygoing—the perfect friend! I live for about 18 years and grow to about 1 foot (30 cm) long. I can be good at talking as well.

Cockatiel

I'm a parakeet! Budgerigars are also parakeets, but there are many different kinds of us, and we all look different. We come in fantastic colors—greens, crimsons, and purples—and have names that sound almost as interesting as we look. I can be any combination of turquoise, crimson, royal blue, baby pink, and sea-grass green. Although I am usually quiet, I have a lovely call and can be a fantastic talker. Treat me with gentleness, and I will be an affectionate companion. I range from 7 to 16 inches (18 to 41 cm) in length. You can expect me to live for 12 to 15 years, though plum-headed parakeets can live as long as 25 years.

Parakeets

Keep Me Safe!

No matter what kind of bird I am, your world can be a dangerous place for me. Here are some ways you can help keep me safe:

▶ Do not use nonstick cookware. It gives off fumes that can make me sick or even kill me! Cleaning products, too, can contain chemicals that could make me very sick.

▶ Find out what kind of climate I need, and do not let me get too cold. I can become very sick if I get chilled.

▶ Keep plants out of my reach. Chewing on the wrong leaves can poison me!

▶ If you let me out of my cage, keep doors and windows closed, and cover windows and mirrors so I won't fly into the glass. Do not set me loose in a room with a fireplace.

Tropical Treasures

I am a parrot—a large bird, packed with talent and personality. Sometimes my personality can be naughty, though! I tend to be loud, squawky, and sometimes rather wild. I can also be very expensive, so I am best suited for the truly dedicated bird lover. Nevertheless, I am very affectionate and make a wonderful companion.

Parrots like me measure about 11 to 15 inches (28 to 38 cm) in length and come in a range of beautiful colors, often warm greens and yellows, that reflect our original tropical homes in the Philippines, Africa, and South America. Blue, purple, and gray are also popular colors. Even our tongues are an interesting color; don't worry, though—they're supposed to be black!

African gray parrot

It is best to get me while I'm young so that you and I can bond. We can have a very special relationship, and my lifespan, as long as 40 years, means that we can be friends for a very long time.

When you talk to me, please speak gently and quietly. If I am calm and comfortable, I can learn tricks like lying down on my back in the palm of your hand. I am very smart and can recognize each member of my human family.

Macaw parrot

Your Fine Feathered Friend

We birds aren't quite as domesticated as other pets. That means that we are not as used to living in homes or with people and still have more of our wild **instincts.** Because of this, a bird like me can sometimes be hard to own. It is very important to do some research before bringing me home. Do you want a little songbird? Do you want a bigger bird, like a parrot, that you will have to feed by hand? Make sure you understand what I need to live safely and comfortably, what I eat, and other information that has to do with my particular bird variety.

Once you have decided on me, you will need to find a good breeder. Many are more concerned with quick breeding than my health. Ask a local veterinarian whether he or she knows of a good breeder.

You'll need to make sure I'm healthy before you bring me home. Pay attention, because when I am sick, I try to hide my illness. This is because in the wild, sick birds are easier prey and are more likely to end up as someone's lunch. There are some signs you can look for, though, to see if I am in good health. I should:

- Be alert.
- Have bright eyes, free of **discharge.**
- Have feathers that look bright and healthy, not worn or picked over.
- Not appear overweight.
- Have all four toes on each claw.
- Not favor one side of my body.
- Breathe without difficulty.

Room to Move

You've heard the phrase "birds of a feather flock together," right? Well, it's certainly true. Like dogs and cats, birds are social animals, so even though I live in a cage, apart from my owner, I still need plenty of attention. Talk, whistle, or sing to me. I cannot live happily without your company.

Keep this in mind when deciding where to put me and my cage. I am generally happiest in the middle of all the action. Keep me in the family room or the living room, where there are sure to be a lot of people. I also love sunlight. Just make sure I don't overheat in the summertime!

While we birds once spent our whole lives in small cages, owners now know that it is better for us—physically and mentally—when you let us out of our cages for short periods of time during the day.

We like to stretch our wings and check out our environment.

You will need to clean up after me, both inside my cage, and sometimes even outside! Dust, feathers, and waste can all stack up pretty quickly, so be prepared, and have plenty of newspaper on hand to line the cage. My living space also needs regular **disinfection.**

Eat Like a Bird

Check with a veterinarian when deciding on a healthy diet and feeding schedule for me. My diet will vary based on my species. Fruits, vegetables, rice, pasta, nuts, meat, and even corn bread or French toast covered with seeds are some of my favorites. Ask the vet about a vitamin or mineral supplement as well.

Body Language

Although I may be able to say "hello" and greet you by name, I do not speak the same language as you. If you learn to read my body language and interpret my squawks, though, you'll see that in my own way I can say so much more.

Staring and Flashing: You can often tell how I'm feeling by paying attention to my eyes. If something scares me, or even delights me, I'll focus on it. Find out what I'm staring at, and it will help you understand my mood. If I'm fluffing up and backing away, maybe I'm scared. Sometimes I quickly open and close the irises of my eyes. This is called **flashing.** I do it when I'm angry. If I'm just looking really intently, I may like what I see.

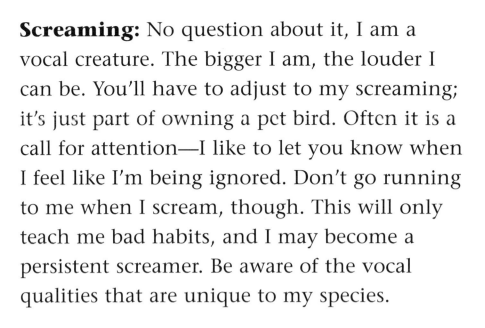

Screaming: No question about it, I am a vocal creature. The bigger I am, the louder I can be. You'll have to adjust to my screaming; it's just part of owning a pet bird. Often it is a call for attention—I like to let you know when I feel like I'm being ignored. Don't go running to me when I scream, though. This will only teach me bad habits, and I may become a persistent screamer. Be aware of the vocal qualities that are unique to my species.

Biting: I also express myself with my beak. I use my beak to say "hello," much the same way that dogs playfully bite one another in greeting. There is a difference, though, between using my beak for greeting and actually biting. Do not allow me to bite!

Clicking and Grinding: If I am clicking my beak, it is likely that I am just restless for attention or want a toy. Grinding the top and bottom of my beak from side to side might sound painful, but I'm really expressing pleasure.

Bird Essentials

As small as I can be, I need a lot of equipment to stay happy and healthy. Here are a few key items:

Identification: In the unfortunate event that I escape, it is good to have an identifying band around my leg.

Cage: Select a cage that is both wide and high enough for me to play inside. Make sure that I am not taller than you when the cage is set up; otherwise, I might think I am in charge. You might find that an additional smaller cage is also useful if you need to punish me, get me out of the way, or travel with me. This might also be a cage to use to give me a shower.

Perch: I need a perch on which to stand. Lots of people make perches from branches outside. Over time, I will destroy a wooden perch. I am not being naughty—this is natural behavior for me. Mineral perches have a scratchy surface. These perches help keep my toenails in check. I am on my perch almost all the time, so it is important that I like it and that it allows me a view of my human family.

Water bottles: A water bottle keeps my water supply fresh, and I can learn to drink from one just like a guinea pig or hamster.

Gym: I like a separate playing area outside my cage with perches, ladders, bells, and lots of room for fun.

Toys: I love to pull things apart. Let me exercise my instincts with pieces of rope, rawhide, or other materials I can destroy. My favorite toys are those that are difficult but not impossible to pull apart. I also like ladders to climb, bells to announce my presence, and mirrors to admire my plumage and keep myself company!

Fun Facts Wings and Things

Sporting Birds

It was once common for people to keep hawks, falcons, and other **raptors** to use for hunting and sport. Today, people called falconers still train these birds to hunt and to perform **aerial** tricks. Their sport is called **falconry.**

Big Birds

Ostriches are enormous at 8 feet (2 meters) tall. They are the largest birds in the world. However, the giant moa of New Zealand was 12 feet (4 m) tall. Unfortunately, this amazing bird has been extinct for about 500 years.

Bird Brain

A parrot's intelligence is on par with 3-year-old children, or dolphins.

The Big Apple

New York City has the largest concentration of peregrine falcons in the entire world! Peregrine falcons are the fastest birds in the world, reaching speeds up to 175 miles (282 kilometers) per hour—that's as fast as the top race cars in the Indianapolis 500!

Itty Bitty Birdy

The smallest bird in the world is called the bee hummingbird, and it comes from Cuba. This bird is only 2¼ inches (6 centimeters) long.

Important Dates Timeline

2000 B.C. — **327 B.C.** — **77 A.D.** — **1493** — **1580** — **1840** — **1861** — **1942** — **1968** — **2004**

2000 B.C. People begin keeping birds as food in ancient civilizations, such as China, Egypt, and India. Realizing how charming birds are, they also begin keeping them as pets.

327 B.C. Alexander the Great receives a bird as a gift after the invasion of Northern India. This bird later becomes known as the Alexandrine parakeet.

77 A.D. In Rome, Pliny the Elder writes what may be the first bird-care book, with advice on how to train parrots to make them talk. The great thinker suggests giving each parrot its own darkened room so it can concentrate.

1493 Columbus brings Queen Isabella of Spain a pair of Cuban Amazon parrots in gratitude for paying for his travels.

1580 Farmers in the Canary Islands are encouraged by the Spanish to sell the native birds we know as canaries to other regions of the world.

1840 Naturalist John Gould brings budgerigars from Australia to England.

1861 The first fossil of the Archaeopteryx dinosaur is found. Many consider these fossils early proof that birds are the direct descendants of dinosaurs.

1942 Tweety Bird, the cartoon canary who spars with Sylvester the Cat in the Looney Toons cartoons, makes his first appearance in "A Tale of Two Kitties."

1968 Big Bird, the cheerful avian puppet, appears on "Sesame Street" for the first time.

2004 Sources announce that Winston Churchill's parrot, Charlie, has been found alive in England at a ripe old age of 104 years. Charlie kept the prime minister company through much of World War II and gained fame for squawking nasty comments about Hitler.

Words to Know

aerial: in or from the air

avian: having to do with birds

aviary: a house for birds

contour feathers: the outer feathers that shape a bird and keep it dry

discharge: a runny fluid

disinfection: deep cleaning to prevent disease

domesticated: accustomed to living with people

downy feathers: soft, fluffy feathers that keep a bird warm

falconry: an activity in which falcons are trained to hunt or perform tricks

flashing: opening and closing the irises quickly

gizzard: a muscular organ in birds where food is broken down

instincts: powerful natural drives

opposable: capable of being placed against one or more of the remaining fingers or toes of a hand or foot

plumage: feathers that cover a bird

radius: a bounded area

raptors: birds of prey

songbirds: birds that have a musical call

Where to Learn More

AT THE LIBRARY

Alderton, David. *You & Your Pet Bird*. New York: Alfred A. Knopf, 1997.

Hamilton, Lynn. *Caring for Your Bird*. Mankato, Minn.: Weigl Publishers, 2003.

Jeffrey, Laura S. *Birds*: *How to Choose and Care for a Bird*. Berkeley Heights, N.J.: Enslow Publishers, 2004.

Spadafori, Gina, and Dr. Brian L. Speer. *Birds for Dummies*. New York: For Dummies, 1999.

ON THE WEB

For more information on birds, use FactHound to track down Web sites related to this book.

1. Go to *www.facthound.com*

2. Type in a search word related to this book or this book ID: 0756507006.

3. Click on the *Fetch It* button.

Your trusty FactHound will fetch the best Web sites for you!

ON THE ROAD

The National Aviary
Allegheny Commons West
Pittsburg, PA 15212
412/323-7235

Look up bird shows and bird expos to find local listings of events selling birds or competitions showcasing birds both large and small.

INDEX

ABOUT THE AUTHOR

Meredith Phillips studied literature and Japanese language at Connecticut College and is near to completing an M.F.A. in creative nonfiction at New School University. She writes about the things she loves—animals, science, books, and food. Her writing has appeared in publications, including *The Believer, The Austin Chronicle,* and *The Columbia Journal.* She also works as an editorial consultant. Meredith lives in Brooklyn, New York.